ENCOURAGING QUOTES
*and* **MESSAGES** *to* **FUEL YOUR**
**LIFE** *with* **POSITIVE ENERGY**

# Stay
# Positive

ON GORDON     DANIEL DECKER

**WILEY**

ISBN 9781119430230 (Hardcover)
ISBN 9781119431053 (ePDF)
ISBN 9781119431046 (ePub)

Printed in the United States of America
F10014648 101819

This book is dedicated to YOU. May the words within it inspire and encourage you to become all you were created to be. We believe in you! The best is yet to come.

# Introduction

"We are not positive because life is easy. We are positive because life can be hard."

—Jon Gordon

This book isn't just a book of positive quotes. It's a resource you can turn to each day to help you improve your life and career by cultivating positive thoughts that help you overcome challenges, negativity, and adversity. The more positivity we develop on the inside, the stronger and more resilient we become in facing the world on the outside. Positivity is a muscle and we can develop it.

It's not about being Pollyanna Positive. It's about the real stuff that makes a proven difference in our perspective and our lives.

*Pessimists don't change the world.*

*Critics write words but they don't write the future.*

*Complainers talk about problems, but they don't solve them.*

Throughout history, we see that it's the optimists, the believers, the dreamers, the doers, and the positive leaders who change the world.

The future belongs to those who believe in it and have the belief, re-silience, positivity, and optimism to overcome all the challenges in order to create it.

That's you.

But this isn't just about you. When we develop positivity within ourselves, we can share it and impact others.

This book and the thoughts within it are meant to be shared.

Our hope is that the quotes in this book encourage you and inspire you to encourage others. We filled this book with a series of inspirational messages that you can read anytime you need a boost. You can start from the beginning or open the book randomly to any page and find a message that speaks to you.

There is a power in positivity. Let's start fueling up with it today!

—Jon and Daniel

# 5 WAYS TO BE MORE POSITIVE

1. Count your blessings. You can't be stressed and thankful at the same time.

2. See your challenges as opportunities for growth.

3. Don't listen to your negative thoughts.

4. Feed yourself with positive encouragement.

5. Choose faith instead of fear.

Three things you control
every day are your
ATTITUDE, your EFFORT,
and your ACTIONS. It
doesn't matter what
others are doing or who
you think is being unfair.
Every day you can focus
on being positive, working
hard, and making others
around you BETTER.

# 6 WAYS TO GET BETTER

1. Be humble and hungry.

2. Focus on your strengths and what matters most.

3. Tune out distractions.

4. See life and people as teachers you can learn from each day.

5. Help others get better.

6. Care more. Put more time, effort, and passion into your work and life.

I heard that on average one person will influence 80,000 people in the course of their life—enough to fill a stadium. But remember, even if you influence just one person you are a leader! Choose to be a positive leader and make a positive impact.

Positive leaders are great encouragers, which is something the world needs more of. With so many people telling us we can't succeed, we need to hear people telling us we can.

**Tell someone you believe in them today.**

Great leaders don't **SUCCEED** because they're great. They succeed because they bring out the **GREATNESS** in others.

**GREATNESS** isn't achieved by worrying what everyone thinks of you. Don't look outside. The praise, criticism, expectations—it's all just noise. Look inside to your **HEART** and soul and do your thing. Do it with **LOVE** and create greatness from the inside out.

**Don't let negativity win today.**

Remember, it starts with you. If you are complaining you're not leading. If you are leading, you're not complaining. One person can't make a team but one person can break a team. Stay positive! No energy vampires allowed.

"

Now more than ever it is a time for action. It is a time for getting things done. It is a time to tune out the distractions and the noise from the doomsayers and the naysayers and focus on what truly matters and what truly will help you create success.

"

God has something great for you but **YOU MUST TAKE ACTION** with faith and go through a battle to seize it. It's never going to be easy. It's not supposed to be. The struggle builds your character, fosters humility, develops your strength, and makes you appreciate the **JOURNEY.**

# 5 Fs FOR TEAM SUCCESS

1. **F**ight: for each other.

2. **F**aith: keep believing.

3. **F**un: enjoy it.

4. **F**ocus: tune out distractions.

5. **F**inish: strong.

Today, shift your perspective and realize it's not about having to do anything. Life is not an obligation. It's a gift. Replace **Have to** with **Get to.** Focus on gratitude and you'll find yourself feeling blessed instead of stressed.

**Everyone says you can't.**
Until you do. Then everyone
wants to know the key to your
success. The key is you don't
listen to everyone.

You have a choice. You can complain about things you can't control or **YOU CAN CONTROL WHAT YOU CAN CONTROL** and let go of what you can't. You can focus on your problems or focus on getting better. You can look for an excuse or you can look within and find your best.

It's a challenge to stay positive on your worst day and humble and hungry on your best day but this will help you keep going and growing.

• • • • • •

If you believe your best days are behind you, they are. If you believe your best days are ahead of you, they are.

# 2 KEYS TO HELP YOU BE YOUR BEST

1. Failure is not meant to define you; it's meant to refine you. Sometimes you have to lose a goal to find your destiny.

2. Ignore the critics. Show up and do the work. You are here for a reason. You have a purpose and you are meant to share it.

Don't focus on the past, and don't look to the future. **FOCUS ON THE NOW.** Success, rewards, accolades, fame, and fortune are merely by-products for those who are able to **SEIZE THE MOMENT**— not those who look beyond it.

The culture of your team will only be as strong as your relationships and commitment to one another.

(From *The Power of a Positive Team*)

A big part of positive leadership and grit is knowing that you will fail along the way. It doesn't define you; it refines you. Just keep moving forward.

Leadership is knowing that the critics will criticize you while still saying what needs to be said and doing what needs to be done. History doesn't remember the critics. It remembers the one who withstood criticism to accomplish something great.

▲●▼

Ignore the critics. Show up, lead the way, and do the work. **Repeat tomorrow!**

> **People often say that adversity makes you stronger, but that's not always true. Many face adversity and become fearful and fragile as a result. The truth is adversity makes you stronger if you learn from it, stay positive and resilient, and use it as fuel for your growth.**

Do it for the cause.

**Not the applause.**

Failure is not meant to define you. It's meant to **REFINE** you to be all you are meant to be. Don't let your failures be a part of your identity. Move forward and create your **FUTURE**.

Positive leaders don't lead in a sea of tranquility but through storms of adversity. That's why optimism, belief, and faith are essential.

• • • • • • •

Leaders don't complain. Once you complain, you are creating a culture that says complaining is the norm, because the leader not only allows it, but practices it. Emotions are contagious, and as a leader, you set the tone for your team.

(From *The Power of a Positive Team*)

Through adversity we have a choice. We can run away from each other or we can run toward each other. Remember: **Connection breeds commitment.**

Don't focus on winning championships, focus on DEVELOPING CHAMPIONS.

When you commit to **something bigger** than yourself, you rise to a level **much higher** than yourself.

Encourage instead of compete.

Many couples seem to be competitive rather than encouraging and supporting each other. Instead of being one team they act like two separate teams and get jealous if their spouse is enjoying success. To have a great relationship you have to be one team who supports and encourages each other. When you support and advocate for each other, you grow as individuals and also strengthen your team.

As a leader your job is to serve, not be served. Your team needs to know you care. Serve their heart. Your team needs to improve. Serve their talent. Your team struggles with doubt. Serve their mind and spirit. Your team has potential. **SERVE THEIR GROWTH.**

> **Teams often break down because of bad communication. They give up because of discouragement, lose momentum because they don't have a vision and purpose, and crumble because of negativity and jealousy. The answer is to become a positive, united, purpose-driven, selfless team.**

If you want to build a winning team, you must value all team members for who they are, not just what they do.

Every person, no matter how successful, wants to be appreciated, respected, and valued. Everyone wants to feel cared about. Everyone, ultimately, wants to be loved.

You are **GREATER** than your circumstances, more **COURAGEOUS** than your fears. The struggle is real but you are strong. Life is tough but you are tougher.

**YOU'VE GOT THIS** and God's got **YOU.**

You know all those struggles you've been through, those times when everything seemed hopeless, when you didn't know how to continue on. They made you stronger, wiser, and better. If you are struggling right now, this is preparing you for growth tomorrow.

What you do does not determine **who you are**. How you perform does not determine your identity. You are a child of God and are loved no matter how you perform. Even if every performance isn't great, you always have **greatness inside you.**

Don't let the pessimists or
the naysayers get you down.
Rise above. Your optimism is a
competitive advantage.

If you do more than expected, you'll
likely accomplish more than what
everyone expects.

Being a positive leader doesn't
just make you better, it makes
everyone around you better.

In a world where you can buy and invest in a lot of things, the greatest investment you can make is in your soul. And the greatest way to invest in your soul is to love God, love yourself, and love others.

# 3 TRUTHS ABOUT LEADERSHIP

1. Leadership isn't about gaining power. It's about empowering others.

2. Great leaders succeed because they bring out the greatness in others.

3. You don't have to be great to serve but you have to serve to be a great leader.

Faith and fear have one thing in common besides the letter F. They both believe in a future that hasn't happened, yet. Fear believes in a negative future. Faith believes in a positive future. If neither has happened, yet why wouldn't we choose to believe in a positive future?

Your team doesn't care if you are a super star. They care if you are a super teammate. You have to work as hard as to be a great team member as you do to be an individual success.

There was a man who traveled to a village to speak to a wise man. He said to the wise man, "I feel like there are two dogs inside me. One dog is positive, loving, kind, and optimistic and then I have this fearful, pessimistic, angry, and negative dog and they fight all the time. I don't know who is going to win." The wise man thinks for a moment and responds, "I know who is going to win. The one you feed the most. **So feed the positive dog.**"

(From *The Positive Dog*)

# 5 WAYS TO LOVE YOUR PASSENGERS TODAY:

**1.** Make time for them.

**2.** Listen to them.

**3.** Recognize them.

**4.** Serve them.

**5.** Bring out the best in them.

(From *The Energy Bus*)

## No Cape Required!

You don't need a special suit, a title, or a superhero name. You just need to tap into the love, spirit, passion, soul, and purpose inside you to create your life and a better world today.

No matter how tired you feel, no matter how much you want to quit, no matter what obstacle is in your way, **keep moving toward** the vision you have for your future.

## BECOME A GRATITUDE MAGNET

When you are grateful for the things in your life, big and small, you always seem to find more things to be grateful about.

Abundance will flow into our life when gratitude flows out of our heart.

# LOVE ALL OF IT

LOVE THE STRUGGLE BECAUSE IT MAKES YOU
APPRECIATE YOUR ACCOMPLISHMENTS.

LOVE CHALLENGES BECAUSE THEY MAKE
YOU STRONGER.

LOVE COMPETITION BECAUSE IT MAKES
YOU BETTER

LOVE NEGATIVE PEOPLE BECAUSE THEY MAKE
YOU MORE POSITIVE.

LOVE THOSE WHO HAVE HURT YOU BECAUSE THEY
TEACH YOU FORGIVENESS.

LOVE FEAR BECAUSE IT MAKES YOU COURAGEOUS.

(FROM THE CARPENTER)

# NO COMPLAINING CHALLENGE

Go a week without complaining about anything and see how it changes your life and team.

Instead of complaining about what you don't have, appreciate what you do have. Instead of complaining about other people, think about something good about them. Instead of complaining about problems, look for solutions. Focus on the positive and help overcome negativity.

Share and invite friends and coworkers to take the challenge too! www.jongordon.com/nocomplaining.

(From *No Complaining Rule*)

Every day, you have a choice of whether you are going to be a shark or a goldfish. Are you going to wait to be fed or go out and find food? It's about learning how to thrive while others merely try to survive. What do you want to be?

(From *The Shark and the Goldfish*)

Navy SEALs say that when you're under pressure you don't

# RISE TO THE OCCASION,

you sink to the level of your training.

# TRAIN WELL!

You can be both **CONFIDENT** and **HUMBLE**. Humble knowing there is a God and it's not you. Confident knowing you were made in God's image and He has a plan for your life.

• • • • • •

Don't let your circumstances alter your faith. Let your faith alter your circumstances.

To thrive under pressure, focus on your love of competing and performing instead of your fear of failing. Focus on the moment, not the outcome.

No one is perfect. **Your past mistakes and failures don't have to define your future.** They can refine you and help you become all that you were created to be. There is a plan for you. You have a purpose. Don't give up. Have faith and continue to get **better.**

Going through the motions won't make an impact. Just showing up doesn't lead to greatness. Michelangelo said, "If people knew how hard I worked to get my mastery, it wouldn't seem so wonderful at all." It's hard to be great. But it's well worth the effort.

Happiness is a by-product of living with passion and purpose. When you live with passion and purpose, happiness will find you.

(From *The Seed*)

> **Without struggle, there would be no triumph. Without setbacks, there would be no feeling of victory and accomplishment. It's all part of the journey!**

Great leadership is really a transfer of belief. Great leaders share their belief, vision, purpose, and passion with others, and in the process they inspire others to believe, act, and impact. Great leaders are positively contagious and they instill confidence and belief in others.

(From *The Power of Positive Leadership*)

Great teams fight. Fighting doesn't make you a bad team. Sometimes you have to have the difficult conversations. Trust, love, and respect are the key. If you have trust, love, and respect, positive conflict will lead to growth.

Commitment always looks like service and sacrifice. Commit to your team (at work and home) by finding ways to serve them and make them better. Start by picking one thing you will do to be a better team member each day. Remember:

# WE>ME

# FOCUS ON THE ROOT, NOT JUST THE FRUIT.

We live in a world where many focus on the fruit of the tree. They focus on the outcome and make decisions based on grabbing the fruit. But if you focus on the fruit and ignore the root, the tree dies. Don't overlook the fundamentals. If you focus on the root, you'll always have a great supply of fruit.

(From *You Win in the Locker Room First*)

A lot of people won't believe in you. Don't blame them. It's not their fault they can't see your **VISION**. Small minds can't understand big **DREAMS**. When you make it, don't say I told you so. Instead just continue to **GROW**.

There's nothing more powerful than a humble person with a warrior spirit who is driven by a bigger purpose.

The more you count **your blessings,**
the less you'll be **stressing.**

"

We are positive, not because life is easy. We are positive because life can be hard. It's not Pollyanna. It's about trusting in God, overcoming obstacles, finding a way forward, and believing the best is yet to come!

"

One person in pursuit of excellence raises the standards of everyone around them. And as they strive for greatness they bring out the greatness, in others.

**Be that one person today.**

To become a truly great leader, you must become a servant leader.

Love. Serve. Care.

(From *The Carpenter*)

Where there is a void in communication, negativity will fill it.

Fill the void with positive, proactive communication and you'll help neutralize the negativity before it starts. This applies at home, at work, and every relationship in your life.

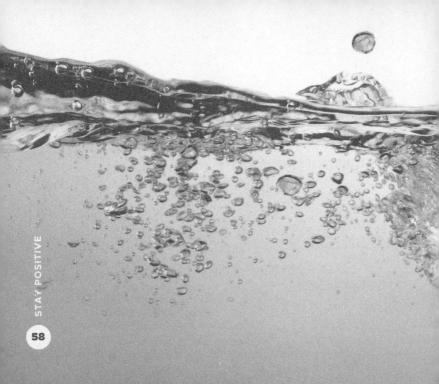

**Mental toughness** is knowing that your identity is not defined by your performanc or outcome. **You are loved no matter what**

No matter what happens today, remember. . .

You might not be able to control all of your circumstances, but you can control how you respond to them.

Pause. Look for the good. Trust in a bigger plan. **Respond instead of react.**

**Don't be afraid to fail when you are striving to be great. It's growth from failures combined with grit, belief, drive, and passion that lead to greatness.**

**A big part of grit is knowing that outside circumstances and people have no power over you. You create your world from the inside out!**

Fear is the number one thing that keeps you from your destiny. But it has no power in the presence of love. Love casts out fear. Fear is weak. Love is strong. Don't fear it. Love it. If you love it you won't fear it.

You aren't a true **success** unless you help others be **successful.**

You may not like your job but you can be thankful you have one. You may have to drive in traffic but thank God you can see while others can't. And while your life may not be where you want it to be, you can believe that the future is bright and great things are happening every day.

Pruning is necessary for growth to happen. What looks bad today leads to greater growth and a harvest in the future. Whatever you are going through, trust that a harvest is coming!

The truth is that to be a better leader, you need to be a better you. Who you are determines how you lead and how you lead determines the culture and team you create.

Gandhi said, "I will not let anyone walk through my mind with their dirty feet," and neither should you.

• • • • • •

We have a daily choice to be negatively contagious or positively contagious. We can be a germ to others or a big dose of vitamin C.

(From *The Power of a Positive Team*)

## LOSS: LEARNING OPPORTUNITY STAY STRONG.

A loss is not the end of the world. It's part of your growth and journey. Decide right now! When I lose, I will come back stronger. When I make mistakes, I will come back better. When I fall down, I will rise up higher.

Don't let the critics stop you. If you
have a dream, keep pursuing it. It
might not happen overnight and you
will likely face challenges along the
way, but keep moving forward. You
were given that desire for a reason.

▲●▼

The future belongs to those who
believe in it and work together
with other positive people in order
to create it.

Today, decide to be that person who instills a positive belief in someone who needs to hear your encouraging words. Believe in others more than they believe in themselves.

> **The character you possess during the drought is what your team will remember during the harvest.**

STAY POSITIVE

Everyone wants to be great but you can't be great without sacrifice. When you lose yourself in the service of a greater cause, you find the greatness within you.

Spread **positive gossip today!**
Be the kind of person who says
**positive things**
about people to other people.

When the enemy knows it can't defeat
you, it tries to get you to defeat yourself.
This goes for your country, your team,
and your life. Stay positive, united,
connected, and encouraged.

Don't worry about your **GREATNESS** in the future. Just be great **TODAY!**

You haven't failed until you stop trying.

When you believe, the impossible becomes **POSSIBLE**. What you believe will become what is true. Your optimism today will determine your level of **SUCCESS** tomorrow. Don't look at your challenges; look up and look to the future. Don't focus on your circumstances. Focus on the right **BELIEFS** that will help you build your success.

Positive energy is like muscle. The more you use it, the stronger it gets. The stronger it gets, the more powerful you become. Repetition is the key, and the more you focus on positive energy, the more it becomes your natural state.

· · · · · ·

It's not your goals that will lead to your success but your **commitment to the process.**

Communication isn't just about speaking. It's also about active listening, listening with the intent to understand and act upon what is being said. Want to improve your relationships and team?

**Be a better listener.**

**Culture** drives expectations and beliefs.
**Expectations** and beliefs drive behaviors.
**Behaviors** drive habits and habits create
the future.

> **The key to success is to be a lifelong learner who continuously works hard to improve.**

> **When you serve in small ways, you get more opportunities to serve in bigger ways.**

Successful people
do ordinary things
with extraordinary
**CONSISTENCY,**
**COMMITMENT,**
and **FOCUS.**

Don't focus on the numbers. **TRUST THE PROCESS.** When you keep doing things the right way, eventually the numbers will rise, the wins will come, and the outcome will happen.

# GREAT LEADERS . . . .

- SMALL EGO, BIG MISSION.

- WE BEFORE ME.

- A LOT OF LOVE AND ACCOUNTABILITY.

- A LOT OF GRACE AND TRUTH.

- DEMANDING BUT NOT DEMEANING.

- LOVING BUT NOT ENABLING.

- SHOUT PRAISE. WHISPER CRITICISM.

- HIGH STANDARDS, LOW TOLERANCE

  FOR EXCUSES.

Activity does not
mean achievement.

Focus on the things
that matter today.

When you **lead with integrity** you won't always win, but you will always do the **right thing.**

Think about all that you worry and stress about. Think about the people you're angry at and the fights you're engaged in. Now remember that one day you will die. It may sound morbid but it's true. In the end how do you want to spend your time and energy? Love more. Fight less.

It doesn't matter how much success you have in your career; if you fail at home you are a failure.

If you don't love it you'll never be great at it. Do what you love and love what you do.

Adversity is not a dead end but a detour to a better outcome than you can imagine!

"

**Being positive won't guarantee you'll succeed. But being negative will guarantee you won't.**

"

Don't tell the world your mission statement. Show the world you are on a mission.

• • • • • •

How you see the world determines the world you see.

(From *The Carpenter*)

**Leaders inspire** and teach their people to **focus on solutions,** not complaints.

Leadership is not just about what you do but what you can inspire, encourage, and empower others to do.

**THOUGHTS ARE MAGNETIC.**

What we think about
we attract.

We don't get burned out because of what we do. We get burned out because we forget why we do it. **Purpose keeps you fresh.**

**Positivity** is like a boomerang. The more we put it out there, the more it **comes back to us.**

**Optimism** is a competitive **advantage.**

**The only person** who can limit your possibilities is **you.**

People follow the leader first and the leader's vision second. It doesn't matter if the leader shares a powerful vision; if the leader is not someone who people will follow, the vision will never be realized. As a leader, who you are makes a difference. The most important message you can share is yourself.

## "Rules without relationship leads to rebellion."

Andy Stanley said this and it's one of my favorite quotes. As a leader you can have all the rules you want, but if you don't invest in your people and develop a relationship with them, they will rebel. This applies amazingly to children as well. It's all about relationships.

Instead of being
disappointed
about where you are, be
**OPTIMISTIC**
about where you are
**GOING.**

Your optimism **TODAY** will determine your level of success **TOMORROW**.

· · · · · ·

Don't chase success. Decide to make a difference and success will find you.

(From *The Seed*)

You matter.

You are enough.

Your past doesn't define you unless you let it. Focus on the future.

Being positive doesn't mean you walk around with rose-colored glasses. It means you overcome the thorns.

Your **GREATEST CHALLENGES** often serve as preparation to help you live and share your **GREATEST PURPOSE**

Just as there are diamonds, gold, and oil inside the earth, there is a priceless **TREASURE** inside of you. You are valuable beyond measure and there is greatness inside you. You don't have to chase it. You already have it! You just have to do the work to bring it out and **SHINE**.

When you start your day with gratitude you create a fertile mind and heart that is ready for great things to happen. When you feel blessed, you can't be stressed. Don't worry about the day. Take it on with power and positivity.

Remember, even if someone's life seems perfect from the outside, everyone is struggling with something on the inside. You're not alone.

## RECIPE FOR A MISERABLE LIFE ☹

Focus on what others have and what you don't.

Be jealous of other people's strengths while focusing on your weaknesses.

## RECIPE FOR A HAPPY LIFE ☺

Be thankful for what you have.

Focus on your strengths.

Celebrate the strengths of others.

Positivity is more than a state of mind that makes you feel better. It's a state of action that makes your team and the world better.

• • • • • •

**Remember, we are better together! The more you work together, the more you will accomplish together.**

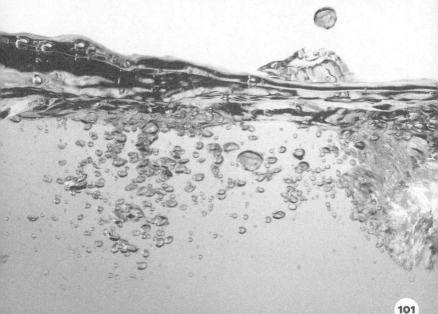

We see failure. God sees **who we are becoming.** We see mistakes. God sees **growth opportunity.** We see where we are now. God sees **where we are going.**

Before you can **achieve it**,
you must **believe it**.

Past success doesn't ensure future
success. Past failure doesn't mean
future failure. The past is gone. It's about
what's next! In any moment you can be
great. Let go of the past. Don't worry
about the future. Seize the moment.

Instead of focusing on the number of "likes," let's invest more in letting people know they are loved.

Don't push someone to greatness. Love them to greatness. When you love them, they'll push themselves.

Being great someday starts with being great TODAY.

You have to be willing to do what most won't do in order to do what most want to do.

**When someone criticizes you, remember this:** I'm not here on Earth for someone else to define me. I am here for God to refine me into what He wants me to be instead of what someone else says I am.

# THREE REMINDERS TODAY.

**1.** You don't have to be perfect to start. Just start.

**2.** Don't be afraid to fail.

**3.** The best is yet to come.

# Be be aware of your thoughts.

Observe your thoughts, keeping in mind that complaints, self-doubt, fear, and negativity lead to unhappiness, failure, and unfulfilled goals over time. When you notice these thoughts, replace the negative with the positive.

Life is meant to be lived forward. Learn from the past but don't live there. Today is a new day to create a better tomorrow.

When you face the naysayers, remember the people who believed in you and spoke positive words to you.

# Talk to yourself instead of listen to yourself

Dr. James Gills is the only person to complete six Double Ironman triathlons, and the last time he did it he was 59 years old.

When asked how he did it, he said, "I've learned to talk to myself instead of listen to myself. If I listen to myself, I hear all the doubts, fears, and complaints of why I can't finish the race. If I talk to myself, I can feed myself with the words I need to keep moving forward."

Fear none of it.

Love all of it.

It's never about the circumstances.
It's always your state of mind and
your thinking that produces how
you feel and respond.

Today, decide to be that person
who instills a positive belief in
someone who needs to hear your
encouraging words.

Your biggest fears are opportunities for your greatest growth.

When we get **excited about life,** we get a life **that is exciting.**

## Celebrate success.

Instead of focusing on what went wrong today, celebrate what went right.

"There will never be peace on Earth until there is peace within us."
—Erwin McManus

Your faith must be bigger than your fear.

Repeat after me:

"Today I will be positively

CONTAGIOUS."

Your plan may not be
**working perfectly,**
but there is a perfect plan
**working in you.**

Culture is a competitive advantage. A team with a great culture seems to have an extra layer of strength, tradition, resilience, belief, and power that makes it **unstoppable!**

Don't get bitter. Get **BETTER.**
Find the lesson and **MOVE ON.**

There is no "i" in team but there are two i's in **POSITIVE.** It means at that "I" must be positive and "I" must help my team be positive to be our best.

The greatest identity theft doesn't come from cybercriminals. It happens when you let what people say on social media define you.

**ABUNDANCE** will flow into your life when **GRATITUDE** flows out of your heart.

Play to win. Commit to yourself that
even if you fail you will never give
up and never let your dreams die.

## KEEP PROMISES TO
## YOURSELF

# Don't let busyness and stress cause you to FOCUS ON what is urgent instead of what is MOST IMPORTANT.

Expect to win today. Champions expect success, and their positive beliefs often lead to positive actions and outcomes. They win in their mind first.

(From *You Win in the Locker Room First*)

**TEAM** beats talent when
**TALENT** isn't a team.

Never do anything out of

obligation. Do everything out of

**GRATITUDE** and **LOVE**.

You are here for a reason.
You have a purpose you are
meant to live and share.

What you think about
matters. Your thoughts
help determine your **reality**.

Speak truth to the lies.
Instead of listening to the negative
lies, choose to feed yourself with
the positive truth.

Fuel up with words, thoughts,
phrases, and beliefs that give
you the strength and power to
overcome challenges and create
an extraordinary life, career, and
team. The truth is that no matter
what is happening around you
and regardless of what negative
thoughts pop into your head, you
possess the capability and power
to take positive action.

# BELIEVE

Read and repeat.

I EXPECT great things to happen today.
I TRUST in God's plan for my life.
I ACCEPT all the love, joy, abundance, and success in my life.
I ACCEPT all the people who want to work with me and benefit from my gifts and talents.
Every day I am getting STRONGER, HEALTHIER, AND BETTER!

(From *The Carpenter*)

Expect challenges, adversity, rejection, and negativity BUT have an even greater expectation that **you will overcome them.**

Remember, it's ALL GOOD.

When you look for the GOOD, expect the GOOD, and see the GOOD, you find the GOOD and the GOOD finds you.

Talk yourself through the fear. Understand that fear is a liar. If you believe the fear-based thoughts you think (I'm not good enough, I'm not smart enough, the world is falling apart), everything around you will validate what you believe to the point where you eventually start to believe it. But know this: Just because you have a negative thought doesn't mean you have to believe it. Don't believe the lie.

The measure of our success will not be determined by how we act during the great times in our life but rather by how we think and respond to the challenges of our most difficult moments.

• • • • • • •

"Every problem has a gift for you in its hands," as Richard Bach says. You can choose to see the curse or the gift. And this one choice will determine if your life is a success story or one big soap opera.

(From *The Energy Bus*)

As a leader, you need to remember it may be work but it's always personal. How you make people feel will determine their level of commitment to you. With your words and actions you want to convey to your team:

- **You belong.**
- **You are safe.**
- **You are loved.**
- **You can trust me.**

FAILURE PROVIDES YOU WITH A GREAT

OPPORTUNITY TO DECIDE HOW MUCH YOU

REALLY WANT SOMETHING. WILL YOU GIVE UP?

OR WILL YOU DIG DEEPER, COMMIT MORE,

WORK HARDER, LEARN, AND GET BETTER? IF

YOU KNOW THAT THIS IS WHAT YOU TRULY WANT,

YOU WILL BE WILLING TO PAY THE PRICE THAT

SUCCESS REQUIRES. YOU WILL BE WILLING TO

FAIL AGAIN AND AGAIN IN ORDER

TO SUCCEED.

Every crisis offers an opportunity to grow stronger and wiser, to reach deep within and discover a better you who will create a better outcome.

No challenge can stop you if you have the courage to keep moving forward in the face of your greatest fears and biggest challenges. **Be courageous.**

Optimism won't guarantee today's victory but it does mean you'll **keep believing** and **working hard** for a better future, giving you a greater chance it will ultimately happen.

**Be an over-believer today!**

Believe in yourself and believe in others. It's amazing what your team will accomplish when you believe in them.

If you want to **CHANGE** your situation you must first change your thoughts. Because if you keep on **THINKING** what you have been thinking, you'll keep on getting what you have been **GETTING.**

Every person and every team will be tested on their journey. It is part of the curriculum of life. It's just like riding a bicycle. In the beginning you're going to fall off and get knocked down, but the important thing is to get back on, stay strong, and after a while you'll master it and ride with the confidence of a champion.

Purpose is the ultimate fuel for our journey through life. When we drive with purpose we don't get tired or bored and our engines don't burn out.

Remember, you have **only one ride** through
life so give it all you got and **enjoy the ride.**

> When you face a setback, think of it as a defining moment that will lead to a future accomplishment.

A leader brings out the best within others by sharing the best within themselves.

Plant yourself like a seed and decide to make a difference where you are and you will grow into the leader and influencer you are meant to be.

When you face negative
people, know that the key
to life is to stay positive in
the face of negativity, not
in the absence of it. After
all, everyone will have to
overcome negativity to
define themselves and
create their success.

Gratitude is like muscle. The more we do with it, the stronger it gets. Make a list of things you are grateful for today.

When you wake up in the morning, take a morning walk of gratitude and prayer. It will create a fertile mind ready for success.

• • • • • •

No one achieves success alone. We all need a team to accomplish great things, and a united and positive team is a powerful team.

Stop scattering your energy and wasting time on trivial things that have nothing to do with your vision and goals and start saying yes to your **PRIORITIES** and to what truly matters. Each day we must make choices, and those **CHOICES** include saying "no" to people and opportunities so we can say "yes" to the work we are meant to do and the **SUCCESS** we are meant to create.

> **When you fail, find the lesson in it, and then recall a time when you have succeeded.**

When you head into **battle,**
visualize **success.**

When you are thinking about the past or worrying about the future, instead focus your energy on the present moment. The now is where your power is the greatest.

When you fear, trust. Let your faith be greater than your doubt.

When you want to complain,
**instead identify a solution.**

• • • • • •

When your own self-doubt
crowds your mind, weed
it and replace it with positive
thoughts and positive self-talk.

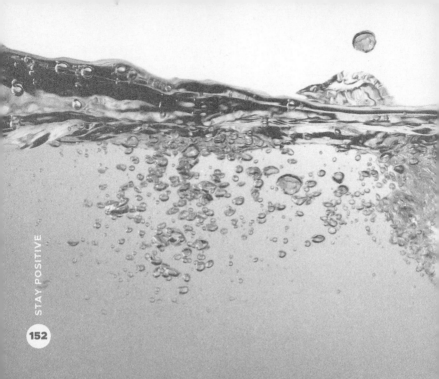

When you feel distracted, focus on your breathing, observe your surroundings, clear your mind, and get into the Zone. **The Zone** is not a random event. It can be created.

When you feel all is impossible, know that with God all things are possible.

When you feel alone, think of all the people who have helped you along the way and who love and support you now.

When you feel lost, pray for guidance.

When you are tired and drained, remember to never, never, never give up.
**Finish strong in everything you do.**

When you feel like your situation is beyond your control, pray and surrender. Focus on what you can control and let go of what you can't.

When you're in a high-pressure situation and the game is on the line and everyone is watching you, remember to smile, have fun, and enjoy it. Life is short; you only live once. You have nothing to lose. Seize the moment.

(From *Training Camp*)

We can take our mess and make it our own message. We can transform our tests into our testimony and our pain can become our purpose to create a better future.

Let go. Focus on the things that you have the power to change, and let go of the things that are beyond your control. You'll be amazed that when you stop trying to control everything, it all somehow works out. Surrender is the answer.

PRAISE OTHERS. INSTEAD OF COMPLAINING ABOUT WHAT OTHERS ARE DOING WRONG, START FOCUSING ON WHAT THEY ARE DOING RIGHT. PRAISE THEM AND WATCH AS THEY CREATE MORE SUCCESS AS A RESULT. OF COURSE, POINT OUT THEIR MISTAKES SO THEY CAN LEARN AND GROW, BUT MAKE SURE YOU GIVE THREE TIMES AS MUCH PRAISE AS CRITICISM.

The world tries to define you by the mistakes of your past. But history defines you by how you responded, how you learned and improved, how you made amends, how you persevered, and what you accomplished afterward.

Don't get stuck thinking that your life can't and won't change for the better. Don't go through life focusing on your problems with your head down. Instead keep your eyes open and your head up. Be open to new possibilities. Be kind to people. Take action. Believe that something great is coming your way. Maintain hope. Believe in what's possible.

# 20 THINGS WE SHOULD SAY MORE OFTEN

The words we speak matter. They help to shape the world around us. That's why I believe we need to speak words of truth and hope, not only to ourselves but to others as well. Here are 20 things we should say more often if we want to make the world more positive:

1. I love you.

2. I believe in you.

3. You are worthy. You deserve it.

4. The best is yet to come.

5. Stay positive.

6. I was wrong. I'm sorry.

7. Please.

8. How can I help?

9. I'm here for you when you want to talk.

10. You can do it.

11. You've got this and God's got you.

12. Please forgive me.

13. I forgive you.

14. I've got your back.

15. I'm open to your feedback. Make me better.

16. You're not alone.

17. Even if we disagree, we can still be friends.

18. You matter.

19. Thank you.

20. There is greatness inside you.

**Stop holding back.** You owe it to yourself and your creator to step into your greatness. It's what you were **born** to do. Anything less will leave you living a life of regret.

**Just start.** You don't need to have it all figured out, you just need to **get started.** One small action today, combined with another tomorrow, gets you closer. No action equals no movement.

Remember, it's bigger than you. Most of the time whatever you're called to do isn't really about you. It's about those whom you will serve. Remember, a message can't get shared unless there is a messenger willing to share it. They need you.

Your circumstances don't define you. Your willingness does. Stop hiding behind the excuses and start stepping into your calling. I believe in you. Now you need to believe in yourself.

• • • • • •

**THE BEST WANT IT MORE.** We all want to be great. But the best of the best are willing to do what it takes to be great. The best don't just think about their desire for greatness; they act on it. They work hard and do the things that others won't do, and they spend more time doing it.

You will always feel fear. Everyone will. But your trust must be bigger than your fear. The bigger your trust, the smaller your fear becomes.

Don't say, "That can't happen."
Don't laugh at the possibility.
Don't feel unworthy. Don't think,
"I don't deserve that." Instead
say, "I'm here for a reason.
There is a plan for my life. Give
me an opportunity and I'll make
the most of it. I don't know
how it will happen, but I trust
that it will. I believe anything is
possible."

You must **BELIEVE** it is possible. You must **DECLARE** it by speaking what you want to be. You must **ACT** on it and create it into existence.

## Show Up.
## Do the Work.

No matter what anyone says, just show up and do
  the work.
If they praise you, show up and do the work.
If they criticize you, show up and do the work.
If no one even notices you, just show up and do the work.
Just keep showing up, doing the work, and leading the way.

Lead with passion.
Fuel up with optimism.
Have faith.
Power up with love.
Maintain hope.
Be stubborn.
Fight the good fight.
Refuse to give up.
Ignore the critics.
Believe in the impossible.
Show up.
Do the work.
You'll be glad you did.
True grit leads to true success.

(From *The Power of Positive Leadership*)

Culture isn't just one thing. It's everything. It's not just one person. It's everyone. Everyone on the team creates the culture. It's your culture. Own it. Make it great.

"I've told my players to let the light inside them always be brighter than the light that's shining on them."
—Coach Dabo Swinney

Expect to win today! When you walk onto the court, onto the field, into a meeting, or into a classroom, expect to win. Expect success and your positive beliefs often lead to positive actions and outcomes. You win in your mind first and then you win in the hearts and minds of your customers, students, or fans.

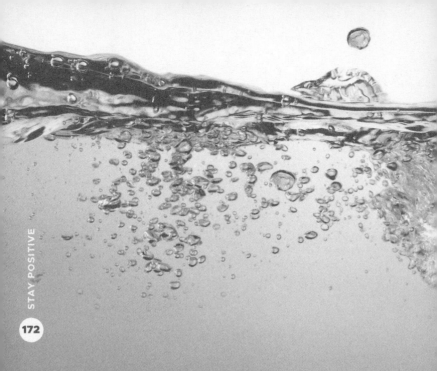

You won't always be recognized for your effort. Do what you do and over time **truth will shine through.**

Remember that the first step to dealing with an energy vampire on your team is to transform them with love, empathy, and coaching. Don't be negative about negativity. Don't sit in the dark with them. Turn on the light.

## Don't make excuses!

Champions don't focus on the faults of others. They focus on what they can do better. They see their mistakes and defeats as opportunities for growth. As a result, they become stronger, wiser, and better.

• • • • • •

No matter how tired you feel, no matter how much you want to quit, no matter what obstacle is in your way, keep moving toward the vision you have for your future. If you can see it, you can create it. If you have a vision, you also have the power to make it happen.

Your power does not come
from your job, uniform, career,
status, circumstance, fame, or
the label people give you.
Your power comes from your
heart, soul, spirit, passion,
and love that exists inside you,
and you are more powerful
than you think.

Be faithful where you are! We all want to be on the big stage, appear on the big TV show, work on the big account, make the big sale, or get the big job right now. But big opportunities and responsibilities come from doing the small things with a big dose of **passion, love, purpose,** and *excellence*.

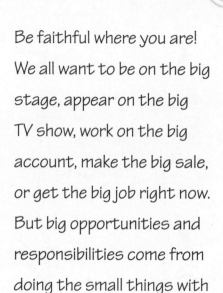

# Don't chase SUCCESS. Decide to get better every day, do great work, and success will find YOU.

STAY POSITIVE

Encourage others today! **So often the difference between success and failure is belief.** Today, decide to be that person who instills a positive belief in someone who needs to hear your encouraging words. Uplift someone who is feeling down. Fuel your team with your positive energy. Rally others to focus on what is possible rather than what seems impossible. Share encouragement. It will help build your relationships. It matters and we all need it.

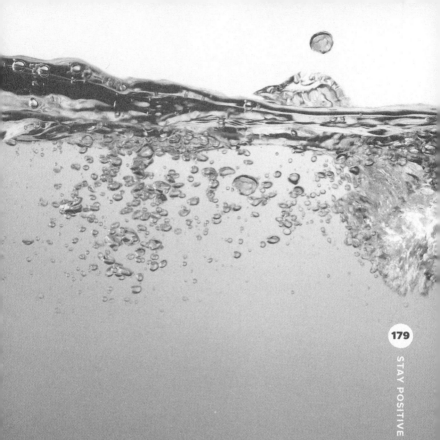

If you want to be great, it's not about **what you can accumulate for yourself,** but rather how much of yourself (your time, your energy, and your talents) **you can give to others.**

To seize the moment, don't let your failure define you; let it fuel you. Let it push you into the moment and beyond yourself. Let it inspire you to live and work each day as though it was your last.

## CARE MORE
## Caring Leads to Success

**CARE** *about the work you do.*
*Surround yourself with people*
*who* **CARE.**
*Show your team you* **CARE**
*about them.*
*Build a team that* **CARES** *about*
*one another.*
*Together show your customers*
*you* **CARE** *about them.*

*(From The Carpenter)*

Weed and feed. Our minds are like a garden; each day you need to weed out the negativity and feed it positivity.

True **LEADERS** don't lead to gain power. They lead to **EMPOWER** and give power away.

Every struggle, every challenge, every failure is meant to help show us **WHO WE ARE** in this moment and how far we have to go to become all we are meant to be. We realize we are unfinished **WORKS OF ART** and our Creator who made us with love is not done with us yet.

It's challenging to work toward a vision and create a positive future. It's difficult to launch new ideas, products, movies, missions, and organizations. It's not easy to pursue greatness and do what has never been done before. **As a team you will face all kinds of adversity, negativity, and tests.** There will be times when it seems as if everything in the world is conspiring against you and your team. There will be moments when you want to give up. There will be days when your vision seems more like fantasy than reality. That's why becoming a positive team is so important. When I talk about positive teams, I am not talking about Pollyanna positivity, where you wear rose-colored glasses and ignore the reality of the situation. Positive teams are not about fake positivity. They are about real optimism, vision, purpose, and unity that make great teams great. Positive teams confront the reality of challenging situations and work together to overcome them.

(From *The Power of a Positive Team*)

**If you want** your team to serve, **serve them.**

**If you want** your people to care, **care about them.**

**If you want** your team to love their work, **love them.**

**If you want** your employees to be their best, **give them your best.**

Failure is not a definition. It's just an event.

You are more powerful than your circumstances. They don't define you.
You do.

# BE THE COFFEE BEAN

Life is often difficult. It can be harsh, stressful, and feel like a pot of boiling hot water. The environments we find ourselves in can change, weaken, or harden us, and test who we truly are. We can be like the carrot that weakens in the pot or like the egg that hardens. Or, we can be like the coffee bean and discover the power inside us to transform our environment.

coffeebeanbook.com

While fear and **WORRY** can weaken or harden you, Love transforms you and the people and situations **around you.**

STAY POSITIVE

No matter how hard things get, or how hopeless things look, **DON'T GIVE UP**. Realize that we don't create our world from the outside in. We **CREATE** and **TRANSFORM** it from the inside out.

# FOCUS ON YOUR MENTAL AND EMOTIONAL FITNESS TODAY!

1. Take a daily gratitude walk.

2. Eliminate complaining and focus on solutions.

3. See every challenge as an opportunity to grow.

Remember, you can't change your past. But you can create your future. Don't get stuck in thinking about what you could have and should have done. Think about what you can and will do and start taking action today!

It's great to learn from the past but don't live there. Say **THANK YOU** to what yesterday taught you and hello to the life you want to create today. Look and live forward. Create a vision of what you want to build, become, and do.

You don't have to wait to feel positive enough for a smile to happen. You can generate a positive feeling by smiling. Your smile can be the source of your positivity, not the result of it.
Smile more today.

The story you tell yourself defines the life you live and the actions you take.
It's important to tell yourself a positive story.

"

**Often the difference between success and failure is belief, and this is often instilled in us by someone who encourages us. Be an encourager today. Be someone who instills a positive belief in others.**

"

Each day when you wake up in the morning, ask the question, "What are the three most important things I need to do today that will help me create the success I desire?" Then each day take action on those three things.

Don't get mad at the naysayers.
Don't hate the energy vampires.
Instead, realize that without them
you wouldn't be as strong. If
you never got sick, you wouldn't
develop a strong immune system.
Negative people make you more
resilient, wiser, and better.

Expect success and you'll find more of it. We get more of what we focus on.

Every day that you choose to work hard and not settle is a day that leads to the life you want.

> **Playing to win requires a commitment to yourself that even if you fail, you will never give up and never let your goals and dreams die.**

> **Move beyond yourself today. Instead of focusing on your problems, focus on helping others with theirs.**

IN LIFE YOU HAVE A CHOICE BETWEEN TWO ROADS, THE POSITIVE ROAD AND THE NEGATIVE ROAD. THE POSITIVE ROAD WILL LEAD TO ENHANCED HEALTH, HAPPINESS, AND SUCCESS AND THE NEGATIVE ROAD WILL LEAD TO MISERY, ANGER, AND FAILURE. CHOOSE THE POSITIVE ROAD TODAY!

Research from the HeartMath Institute (heartmath.org) shows that when you have a feeling in your heart, it goes to every cell in the body, then outward—and other people up to 10 feet away can sense feelings transmitted by your heart. This means that each day you are broadcasting to your team how you feel. You are either broadcasting positive energy or negative energy, apathy or passion, indifference or purpose.

Just as there are diamonds, gold, and oil inside the earth, there is a priceless treasure inside of you. You are valuable beyond measure and there is greatness inside of you. You don't have to chase it. You already have it! You just have to do the work to **bring it out and shine.**

The enemy uses the **triple D** to **divide**, **discourage**, and **destroy**. Don't take the bait. Stay united. Stay encouraged. Stay strong in faith, love, and hope. Remember LOVE wins.

**L**-ove

**O**-ptimism

**V**-ision

**E**-ncouragement

## TELL YOURSELF THESE 5 THINGS TODAY:

**1.** You are loved!

**2.** You matter.

**3.** It's okay to fail. Everyone does.

**4.** Fear is normal. Don't worry about the outcome. Go for it!

**5.** Smile, you've got this.

**LIFE** is about people, commitment, loyalty, and relationships. In the end we won't be **MEASURED** by our bank account, sales numbers, or wins and losses, but by the difference we made in people's lives and the difference we made through **RELATIONSHIPS**.

Remember, most great achievements have humble beginnings. You have to be willing to start small and work hard for a really long time to eventually see big results.

• • • • • •

No one ever regretted dedicating themselves to being their best! We regret what we didn't do knowing we could have done more and become more. **No regrets! Commit now.** Do the work. You'll always feel good knowing you gave your all.

You are greater than your circumstances. More courageous than your fears. The struggle is real but you are strong. Life is tough but you are tougher. You are a child of God and you are loved. Remember this today and every day.

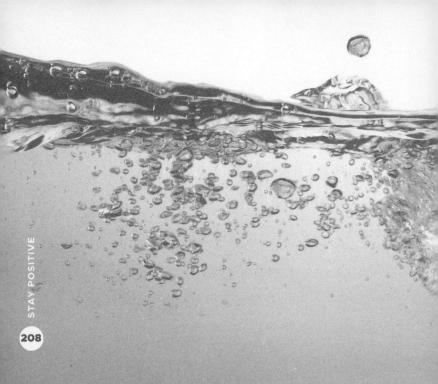

**Culture is not static. It's dynamic.** You can change it by what you say. You can elevate it by what you think. You can improve it by what you share. You can transform it by what you do. You can work to create a positive culture right now.

A thought's power only comes from the power you give it. You don't have to give your negative thoughts power. You can ignore them. You can see them for what they truly are: lies, lies, lies. Just because you have a negative thought doesn't mean you have to believe it.

"

Stop trying to be somebody and instead focus on helping somebody. That's the best way to make a difference.

"

Even when the world is at its worst, you can be at your best. That's how real change happens. We create our world inside out!

You don't **ALWAYS** get what you want. Sometimes God gives you what you need to make you a better **PERSON.**

Life is fragile. We don't
know what tomorrow will
bring. Make the most
of today. Love life. Love
people. Serve others.
CARE MORE.

You have a desire to be great because you were never meant to be average. Don't let fear keep you from becoming all you're meant to be.

Simple rule for a happier life: don't compare yourself to others. Comparison is the thief of joy.

A great way to **make an impact** as a leader is to remind people of the power that exists inside them to **create the world** outside them.

A leader is a **DEALER OF HOPE.** But if you don't have it, you can't share it. It starts with you. What gives you hope? What do you hope for?

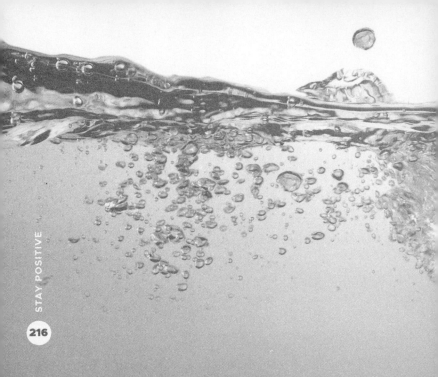

You can't know the joy of living your purpose without the experience of struggling to find it. **Embrace it all.**

Remember that the mountain, no matter how big, is no match for your faith and desire to climb it. Mountains are meant to be climbed. Wounds are meant to be healed and problems are meant to become learning experiences. They all serve a purpose. They make us stronger mentally, emotionally, and spiritually.

## 5 Ways to be a Positive Communicator Today:

1. Shout praise, whisper criticism.
2. Encourage others.
3. Smile more.
4. Don't complain.
5. Welcome feedback.

Our most dangerous critic is the one inside our own head. **Don't listen to the critic.** Listen to your heart, which knows you were born to do this.

Today, don't focus on building your career/business. Focus on *loving, serving,* and *caring* and your career/business will grow exponentially.

Before you go to bed, celebrate your success of the day. Identify the one great thing about your day: the one great conversation, accomplishment, thing that made you smile, or the win that you are most proud of. Focus on your success, and you'll look forward to creating more success tomorrow.

Don't surrender and give up;
surrender and let go of the outcome.

When you serve others in small ways, you get more opportunities to serve in bigger ways. Serving others not only helps others grow, it helps you grow.

Success doesn't always breed success. It often breeds complacency and amnesia as you forget what made you successful in the first place.

Bad things happen to good people. But good people with great optimism, resilience, and faith ultimately turn the bad into good.

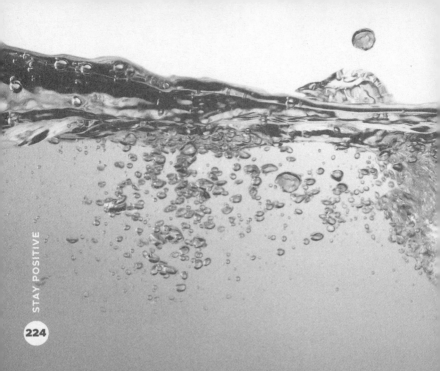

## Grit? What is it?

I believe it's driven by love. Inspired by vision and purpose. Fueled by optimism and belief. Powered by faith and hope. Revived by resilience. Kept alive by stubbornness. And if we're honest, it includes some fear of failure and desire to prove oneself.

It's not easy. It might take longer than you expect. There will be days you question yourself and wonder if it's worth it or if you are on the right path. Trust your gut. Pay your dues. Work hard (and smart) and eventually success will *come.*

Regardless of what you create, someone will hate it. Just remember you didn't create it for them. You created it for the others who love it. Don't let the one distract you from serving the many.

Transactional thinking says, "What can I get?" while relational thinking is more about "What can I give?" Focus on the relationship.

**WE ARE BLESSED TO BE A BLESSING**. This doesn't have anything to do with material things (although it can). It's about having a mind-set of gratitude . . . seeing your life as a gift and using your gifts to make a difference for others.

Speak life to others today. Share a kind word with everyone you interact with. You never know how much their soul might need it.

When you feel called to a vision that you think is not achievable, it's probably not, if you try to do it on your own. Big dreams require us to have faith in a big God to help us accomplish something great.

Often the cost of pursuing your purpose is great. But the cost of not pursuing it is even greater.

Stepping into your destiny often means stepping away from security. **Be bold. Have faith. Take action.**

Don't get consumed with consuming. Consumption never leads to happiness. **TRUE** happiness comes not from what we **GET** but from what we **GIVE**.

## LIVE RICH

You can spend the rest of your life trying to get rich or you can choose to live rich now. Here's how:

1. Do good.

2. Be generous.

3. Share.

> **Don't lower your belief to the level of your circumstance. Stay faithful even when hope seems lost. It may not seem like it today, but there is a greater plan at work in your life.**

STAY POSITIVE

# LIVE AND WORK WITH MERAKI

Meraki. It sounds like it's a Japanese word but it's actually a Greek word and it means to do something with love, creativity, and soul; to leave a piece of yourself in your work; to leave something behind.

Put your love and soul into it.

Leave a piece of yourself in whatever it is you are building. Create a masterpiece that reflects the essence of your love, energy, effort, and craft.

What you focus on in life determines whether you will experience peace in your heart. Today, focus on what you have, **NOT** what you don't.

Often the biggest competitor for our hearts is the stuff that's in our hands. Be careful not to value **THINGS** more than **PEOPLE.**

It's not always the
## smartest or the strongest
who win. It's the ones who are the
## most willing.

# EVERYONE MATTERS

1. Recognize and celebrate their unique gifts and potential.

2. Call them up by challenging them to become all they were created to be.

3. Affirm their worth, tell them that they are part of a bigger plan and that they are loved.

Be so invested in your craft that you don't have time to listen to the naysayers. No time for negativity. Too busy creating your future!

A promise to yourself is just as important as a promise to others. If you tell yourself you're going to do something, don't give up on it. Your promises matter.

Tomorrow is a new day. Don't let what you didn't do become what you never did. No more putting it off. No more waiting till the "perfect" time. No more letting busyness get in the way. **Get started.**

Become the CEO of your life: the Chief Elimination Officer. Say no to good things so you can say YES to the great things.

# Success
## of any kind
## starts in your mind.
# Perspective
# matters.
## Opportunity is everywhere,
## if you choose to
# SEE IT.

An original is way more valuable than a replica. When you try to be like everyone else you get lost in the sea of mediocrity. Instead, embrace what makes you unique.

Be a great you!

**STAND OUT!**

If you don't believe in miracles, remember that you live on a giant liquid rock traveling through space 60,000 mph around the sun. You can try to be logical but there's nothing logical about our existence. **Life is a miracle.** You are a miracle.

*Commitment recognizes commitment! Don't wait for others to commit to you. Decide to commit to them. You be the committed one and watch how it impacts your team's commitment.*

John Wooden didn't win his first national title until his 16th season at UCLA. Success takes time. Starbucks did not reach store number 5 until 13 years into its history. Success takes time. Sam Walton did not open his second store until 7 years after starting his company. Success takes time. Be persistent. Success will come.

Your **thoughts** determine your actions and your actions determine your results.

# Think big.

Don't focus on proving
the naysayers wrong.

Focus on proving God
right. You were born
to do this!

## TODAY I WILL

**1.** Attack this day with enthusiasm.

**2.** Stay positive.

**3.** Be thankful.

**4.** Learn, improve, grow.

**5.** Be a blessing to others.

The goal in life is not to be better than anyone else. It's to be better today than you were yesterday.

Remember, if it was easy you wouldn't be as strong!

Don't waste energy on things you can't control. Focus on what you can control, such as getting better and making others around you better.

Knocked down but not beaten. Tired but not giving up. I saw the sun peek through the clouds. Sometimes all we need is a **glimmer of hope.**

No matter how hard we work and how much we improve, there will be times when we experience the worst of defeats instead of the greatest of victories. But ultimately life is about more than winning or losing. It's about the lessons we learn, the character and strength we build, and the people we become along the way.

# 5 THINGS TO DO INSTEAD OF COMPLAIN

1. **Practice Gratitude.** Research shows that when we count three blessings a day, we get a measurable boost in happiness that uplifts and energizes us. It's also physiologically impossible to be stressed and thankful at the same time. Two thoughts cannot occupy our mind at the same time. If you are focusing on gratitude, you can't be negative. You can also energize and engage your coworkers by letting them know you are grateful for them and their work.

2. **Praise Others.** Instead of complaining about what others are doing wrong, start focusing on what they are doing right. Praise them and watch as they create more success as a result. Of course, point out their mistakes so they can learn and grow, but make sure you give three times as much praise as criticism.

3. **Focus on Success.** Start a success journal. Each night before you go to bed, write down the one great thing about your day. The one great conversation, accomplishment, or win that you are most proud of. Focus on your success, and you'll look forward to creating more success tomorrow.

4. **Let Go.** Focus on the things that you have the power to change, and let go of the things that are beyond your control. You'll be amazed that when you stop trying to control everything, it all somehow works out. Surrender is the answer.

5. **Pray.** Scientific research shows that daily prayer reduces stress; boosts positive energy; and promotes health, vitality, and longevity. When you are faced with the urge to complain or you are feeling stressed to the max, stop, be still, plug-in to the ultimate power, and recharge.

(From *The No Complaining Rule*)

Faith and perseverance turn a dead end into a detour to a better outcome than you ever thought possible.

Expecting to win without hard work and preparation is arrogance. Expecting to win because you have prepared and worked hard is confidence.

If you have talent, the world is waiting for you to share it. Don't let fear stop you. Don't wait for someone to tell you that you are worthy. Stop telling people that you are waiting for someone to discover you. Just start sharing your gifts and use all the technologies available to create your own audience.

You don't have to be **GREAT** to serve, but you have to **SERVE** to be great.

Believe in others more than they believe in themselves and you will be more than a coach/manager/leader. You will be a transformer of lives.

Great coaches, teachers, and mentors see potential rather than limitations. **Look for the good in others today.**

Every day we face challenges, fears, obstacles, and negativity that hit us with left jabs and right hooks. We get so caught up in the details of bills, job pressures, raising kids, fixing the house, car payments, trying to make a living, and a hundred other to-dos, that we can't even see over the piles of paper on our desk, let alone our future success. But when times are tough and your bills are bigger than the balance in your checking account, or when your business has slowed down and you're not sure what to do next, or when your future is uncertain and all feels hopeless—these are the times when you need to realize the most that you are part of a bigger plan. There is greatness in you. There is a big life plan for you.

# Rejection is often our greatest protection.

Sometimes not getting what we want leads us to getting what **WE NEED.**

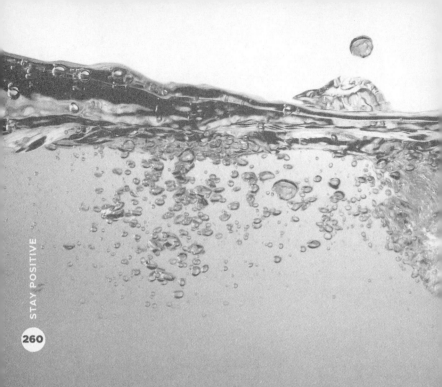

The enemies of great leadership are **busyness and stress.** They keep us from caring about the people we are supposed to care about. **Focus on your people today**

> Don't let fear get in the way of the life that is meant for you. Einstein, Beethoven, Muhammad Ali, and Helen Keller show us that anything is possible. They are real people who overcame their obstacles and doubters and discovered their greatness. So can you.

> You will always feel fear. Everyone will. But your trust must be bigger than your fear. The bigger your trust, the smaller your fear becomes. And the more you trust, the more you become a conduit for miracles.

Today I want to encourage you to do some digging. Think about what's holding you and your team back. What needs to be unearthed and dealt with? I know it's easier not to address or confront it, but remember the law of the skyscraper. If you don't dig you'll never be able to build the foundation you need to create the life and team that you want.

## Quit for the right reasons.

Don't quit because work is hard or you're experiencing challenges. Quit because in your heart you know there is something else for you to do. Quit because you are not benefiting yourself or the organization you work for. Quit because you are absolutely certain you are no longer supposed to be there.

• • • • • •

## The quest for your purpose is not a straight line. It is filled with

mystery, signs, obstacles, victories, dead ends, delays, and detours. Your job is to stay optimistic and faithful on your quest.

Talent isn't enough. Talent doesn't last. It will only take you so far. Talent without character is like an expensive car with no gas. It's useless without the fuel that drives it. Character drives talent toward greatness. A person who is humble, hungry, hard working, honest, dedicated, selfless, loyal, passionate, and accountable will be the kind of person who develops their talent and makes the right decisions to benefit themselves and the team. Character guides and drives your team members to be their best and to bring out the best in others.

The truth is that numbers and goals don't drive people. People with a purpose drive the numbers and achieve goals. Research clearly shows that true motivation is driven by meaning and purpose rather than extrinsic rewards, numbers, and goals.

*Success* is often measured by comparison to others. *Excellence*, on the other hand, is all about being the best we can be and maximizing our gifts, talents, and abilities to perform at our highest potential. We live in a world that loves to focus on success and loves to compare. We are all guilty of doing this. However, I believe that to be our best we must focus more on excellence and less on success. We must focus on being the best we can be and realize that our greatest competition is not someone else but ourselves.

Our happiness comes not from the work we do but from how we feel about the work we do. Remember, happiness is an inside job!

"

**Make a difference in the lives of the people in front of you. Don't look past them to see your destination. Realize the people in front of you are the ones who will lead you to your destination.**

"

Love is what separates good and great. Good teachers know their lesson plans. Great teachers also know and love their students. Good coaches know X's and O's. Great coaches also know and love their players. Good salespeople know how to sell. Great salespeople also love their clients. Good leaders know their vision and purpose. Great leaders also know and love their people. It's simple. Greatness is built with love.

# 20 WAYS TO GET MENTALLY TOUGH AT WORK, IN SPORTS, AND LIFE

1. When you face a setback, think of it as a defining moment that will lead to a future accomplishment.

2. When you encounter adversity, remember, the best don't just face adversity; they embrace it, knowing it's not a dead end but a detour to something greater and better.

3. When you face negative people, know that the key to life is to stay positive in the face of negativity, not in the absence of it. After all, everyone will have to overcome negativity to define themselves and create their success.

4. When you face the naysayers, remember the people who believed in you and spoke positive words to you.

5. When you face critics, remember to tune them out and focus only on being the best you can be.

6. When you wake up in the morning, take a morning walk of gratitude and prayer. It will create a fertile mind ready for success.

7. When you fear, trust. Let your faith be greater than your doubt.

8. When you fail, find the lesson in it, and then recall a time when you have succeeded.

9. When you head into battle, visualize success.

10. When you are thinking about the past or worrying about the future, instead focus your energy on the present moment. The now is where your power is the greatest.

11. When you want to complain, instead identify a solution.

12. When your own self-doubt crowds your mind, weed it and replace it with positive thoughts and positive self-talk.

13. When you feel distracted, focus on your breathing, observe your surroundings, clear your mind, and get into the Zone. The Zone is not a random event. It can be created.

14. When you feel all is impossible, know that with God all things are possible.

15. When you feel alone, think of all the people who have helped you along the way and who love and support you now.

16. When you feel lost, pray for guidance.

17. When you are tired and drained, remember to never, never, never give up. Finish strong in everything you do.

18. When you feel like you can't do it, know that you can do all things through Him who gives you strength.

19. When you feel like your situation is beyond your control, pray and surrender. Focus on what you can control and let go of what you can't.

20. When you're in a high-pressure situation and the game is on the line, and everyone is watching you, remember to smile, have fun, and enjoy it. Life is short; you only live once. You have nothing to lose. Seize the moment.

(From *Training Camp*)

When fear is keeping you from doing something you know you are meant to do, then you have an even greater reason to do it. Because when you conquer your greatest fears you are able to **live and share your greater purpose.**

When you are fearful, stressed, or putting pressure on yourself, remember that one day you will die. You don't do this to become more fearful. You do this to become more focused:

- To enjoy your life.

- To make the most of today.

- To do what matters most.

- To fearlessly go for it.

- To not waste time on trivial things.

- To live without regrets.

## *Other Books by Jon Gordon*

### The Energy Bus

A man whose life and career are in shambles learns from a unique bus driver and set of passengers how to overcome adversity. Enjoy an enlightening ride of positive energy that is improving the way leaders lead, employees work, and teams function.

www.TheEnergyBus.com

### The No Complaining Rule

Follow a VP of Human Resources who must save herself and her company from ruin and discover proven principles and an actionable plan to win the battle against individual and organizational negativity.

www.NoComplainingRule.com

### Training Camp

This inspirational story about a small guy with a big heart, and a special coach who guides him on a quest for excellence, reveals the eleven winning habits that separate the best individuals and teams from the rest.

www.TrainingCamp11.com

### The Shark and the Goldfish

Delightfully illustrated, this quick read is packed with tips and strategies on how to respond to challenges beyond your control in order to thrive during waves of change.

www.SharkandGoldfish.com

### Soup

The newly appointed CEO of a popular soup company is brought in to reinvigorate the brand and bring success back to a company that has fallen on hard times. Through her journey, discover the key ingredients to unite, engage, and inspire teams to create a culture of greatness.

www.Soup11.com

### The Seed

Go on a quest for the meaning and passion behind work with Josh, an up-and-comer at his company who is disenchanted with his job. Through Josh's cross-country journey, you'll find surprising new sources of wisdom and inspiration in your own business and life.

www.Seed11.com

### One Word

*One Word* is a simple concept that delivers powerful life change! This quick read will inspire you to simplify your life and work by focusing on just one word for this year. *One Word* creates clarity, power, passion, and life-change. When you find your word, live it, and share it, your life will become more rewarding and exciting than ever.

www.getoneword.com

### The Positive Dog

We all have two dogs inside of us. One dog is positive, happy, optimistic, and hopeful. The other dog is negative, mad, pessimistic, and fearful. These two dogs often fight inside us, but guess who wins? The one you feed the most. *The Positive Dog* is an inspiring story that not only reveals the strategies and benefits of being positive, but also an essential truth: being positive doesn't just make you better; it makes everyone around you better.

www.feedthepositivedog.com

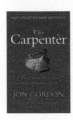

### The Carpenter

*The Carpenter* is Jon Gordon's most inspiring book yet—filled with powerful lessons and success strategies. Michael wakes up in the hospital with a bandage on his head and fear in his heart after collapsing during a morning jog. When Michael finds out the man who saved his life is a carpenter, he visits him and quickly learns that he is more than just a carpenter; he is also a builder of lives, careers, people, and teams. In this journey, you will learn timeless principles to help you stand out, excel, and make an impact on people and the world.

www.carpenter11.com

### The Hard Hat

A true story about Cornell lacrosse player George Boiardi, *The Hard Hat* is an unforgettable book about a selfless, loyal, joyful, hard-working, competitive, and compassionate leader and teammate, the impact he had on his team and program, and the lessons we can learn from him. This inspirational story will teach you how to build a great team and be the best teammate you can be.

www.hardhat21.com

### You Win in the Locker Room First

Based on the extraordinary experiences of NFL Coach Mike Smith and leadership expert Jon Gordon, *You Win in the Locker Room First* offers a rare, behind-the-scenes look at one of the most pressure-packed leadership jobs on the planet, and what leaders can learn from these experiences in order to build their own winning teams.

www.wininthelockerroom.com

### Life Word

*Life Word* reveals a simple, powerful tool to help you identify the word that will inspire you to live your best life while leaving your greatest legacy. In the process, you'll discover your *why*, which will help show you how to live with a renewed sense of power, purpose, and passion.

www.getoneword.com/lifeword

### The Power of Positive Leadership

*The Power of Positive Leadership* is your personal coach for becoming the leader your people deserve. Jon Gordon gathers insights from his bestselling fables to bring you the definitive guide to positive leadership. Difficult times call for leaders who are up for the challenge. Results are the by-product of your culture, teamwork, vision, talent, innovation, execution, and commitment. This book shows you how to bring it all together to become a powerfully positive leader.

www.powerofpositiveleadership.com

### The Power of a Positive Team

In *The Power of a Positive Team*, Jon Gordon draws upon his unique team building experience, as well as conversations with some of the greatest teams in history, to provide an essential framework of proven practices to empower teams to work together more effectively and achieve superior results.

www.PowerOfAPositiveTeam.com

### The Coffee Bean

From bestselling author Jon Gordon and rising star Damon West comes *The Coffee Bean*: an illustrated fable that teaches readers how to transform their environment, overcome challenges, and create positive change.

www.coffeebeanbook.com

### The Energy Bus for Kids

The illustrated children's adaptation of the bestselling book *The Energy Bus* tells the story of George, who, with the help of his school bus driver, Joy, learns that if he believes in himself, he'll find the strength to overcome any challenge. His journey teaches kids how to overcome negativity, bullies, and everyday challenges to be their best.

www.EnergyBusKids.com

### Thank You and Good Night

*Thank You and Good Night* is a beautifully illustrated book that shares the heart of gratitude. Jon Gordon takes a little boy and girl on a fun-filled journey from one perfect moonlit night to the next. During their adventurous days and nights, the children explore the people, places, and things they are thankful for.

### The Hard Hat for Kids

*The Hard Hat for Kids* is an illustrated guide to teamwork. Adapted from the bestseller *The Hard Hat*, this uplifting story presents practical insights and life-changing lessons that are immediately applicable to everyday situations, giving kids—and adults—a new outlook on cooperation, friendship, and the selfless nature of true teamwork.

www.HardHatforKids.com

### One Word for Kids

If you could choose only one word to help you have your best year ever, what would it be? *Love? Fun? Believe? Brave?* It's probably different for everyone. How you find your word is just as important as the word itself. And once you know your word, what do you do with it? In *One Word for Kids*, bestselling author Jon Gordon—along with coauthors Dan Britton and Jimmy Page—asks these questions to children and adults of all ages, teaching an important life lesson in the process.

www.getoneword.com/kids